Body My House

Body My House

POEMS

Bethany Reid

Goldfish Press
Seattle

Published by Goldfish Press
4545 42nd Avenue Southwest
Suite 211
Seattle, WA 98116-4243

Manufactured in the United States of America

ISBN – 13: 978-0971259812
ISBN – 10: 097125981X

Library of Congress Card Number: 2018941254

Cover photo, "Eclipse's First Snow," by Ellen Felsenthal
Photograph of the author by Francine Walls

for my mother

and for her granddaughters

Contents

Foreword

1. Unbridled

The Soul Has Seasons   3
Contract with the Body   4
Eve, Unclothed   5
Where She Lies Down   6
The Body Stands Waiting   7
Unbridled   8
Hound   9
Hasn't Marriage a Soul?   10
Her Desk   11
What Clutter Does   12
Griffin   13
Unripened   14
If I'm Not   16
I Could Love You That Way   17

2. Take Heart

She wakes to find her heart   21

3. Living in Books

To Begin   37
Into the Ice   38
Like Protecting Wings   39
Fabled   40
Insomnia   41
English Café   42
If Plot Is What Happens   43
Invitation   44
When Poems Sit Vacant   45

What She Wanted to Put in Her Poem   46
Marrying the Villain   47
Living in Books   48
Why We Write   50

4. What World, in Our Becoming

Sleep   53
What World, in Our Becoming   54
How Stories Go   55
The Soul, Lifting   56
Her Dream of Winter   57
When He Thought of Peace   58
Legs Thin as Branches   59
What Didn't Happen   60
What I Need Now   62
Her Heart, Her Soul   63

Acknowledgments   65

Foreword

The poems in *Body My House*, Bethany Reid's numinous fourth book of poems, ground themselves in the body and take flight from the body. They are intimate, searing, and startling in their metaphorical transformations. In one poem Reid writes:

Damp as a bunker, her heart
is a room of old books
              ("Take Heart")

and in another:

Like a hunter keeps hounds,
I keep a string of angers
chained in a muddy side yard.
              ("Hound")

Here are perceptive and witty poems about marriages in various states of disintegration (one between a lion and a mouse is particularly funny), houses ("Jars of tomatoes/arranged on a shelf"), and horses ("dreams that will ride us bareback"). They are full of eagles and swans and goats and strawberries and wine and "blue rhymes." They are also full of crumpled coffee cups, cellophane wrappers, spent cigarettes. Time—the sort of time a poet has while raising three children—is "an unfriended beast." She "sways in a corner,/ red eyes oozing."

Reid's poems, especially here, are in the tradition of the great poet May Swenson, and they pay homage to Swenson, whose "Body my house/ my horse my hound/ what will I do/ when you are fallen" frames the stunning work you hold in your hands. These are poems to read and reread, and to savor.

—Priscilla Long, Seattle, Washington, 2018

1. Unbridled

Body my house
my horse my hound
what will I do
when you are fallen

—May Swenson

The Soul Has Seasons

Like blackberry brambles the soul has seasons
when its leaves grow scarce.

Even then, a smallish body will find shelter there,
deer mouse chittering, or the tiny wren, piping its song.

For what, if not that singing, does the soul dare
a new season's greening?

Contract with the Body

Today I chronicle the pleasures
of the body. Each ache, the headache
I woke with last night, I now
recite. Its throb in my socket,
the hand across my eyes as I pressed
myself back into sleep. I accept
the cramp, the scraped knuckle,
every toe ever stubbed.
For all of these, I give thanks.
For crow's feet, for cellulite,
for the belly and thigh, for split ends.
For the child whose bicycle tire
slammed into my shin then ran
over my foot, for the slammed shin
and bruised foot. For the child herself,
I give thanks. For the traffic light.
For the rain. For my car heater
which blows only cold air. For the boy
on the black and chrome motorcycle
who swerves into my lane. For the
stitch in my back, for the hitch
in my knee, for the gut's rumble,
flare of a rash. The rushed heart,
irregular periods, fading eye.
The mammogram. The hangnail.
Each new freckle I scratch across
the register of my years. I turn none
of it back. Even what I forget
and the curse because I forgot,
I welcome as evidence of breath.
I write all of it down.
Because you are gone, I chronicle the body
and call it pleasure. I don't forget you.

Eve, Unclothed

Flesh was the first consequence of sin.
Before her teeth crunched
through that crisp skin,
Eve wore her body like a cloak.
Adam when he kissed her,
kissed not lips, not belly, not neck,
not her ankle, not her sex—
he kissed her watery, exquisite soul.
Nibbling, it was flesh
she turned to, her body
no longer like wind in trees,
no longer the snake's transparent shedding.
It became the lion's fur, leather back
of the gila, inseparable from what
she thought as *self*
as screech from owl, as howl
from wolf. She could no longer
throw her body down
and walk, immaterial, with her god,
invisible, the nucleus inside the atom,
not-Adam and not-Eve, but flesh, clay,
remnant of Eden's long, last day.

Where She Lies Down

She builds a house of cardamom and ginger,
of the licorice child-bite of anise. She builds
        cabinets of old sleds, beds of baskets
and elbow pipes. Who

    would lie here? What house can rise
above walls of sugar-frosted violets?
        Her house isn't sweet-n-low, isn't candied over.
She builds it of sages, a house so bitter

        its windows break like teeth in wartime.

Her sons go for soldiers. Her daughters
gather baskets of salt, wear purple hearts
        on their sleeves. What house is this
where her forehead vaults,

where her neck arches, where her shoulders
        block the eye of the sky?

The Body Stands Waiting

Both soul and heart,
without the body's firm stanchions
grow pale. The body
like a housewife opens its blinds
to let in the light. What is not
the body must offer gifts
to entice the body.
Soul offers strawberries and wine,
the silhouette of mountains at sunset.
Heart offers another body
with its steady pulse of thirst,
its awkward hungers
and shaky embrace.
Thinking itself a god, body sits
at soul's table. It feasts on the heart,
stabbing its fork into every happiness.
It makes suffering its dessert.
What is heaven, if not what Corinthians
tells us, a doling out
of all things done in the body?
Comic or tragic,
here trudges the body to judgment,
stripped and cleansed, its sins
laid in its arms
like a fresh suit of clothes.

Unbridled

after James Wright's "A Blessing"

On a late winter day, I visit a friend's five acres
to meet her new filly.
Eclipse is a rescue from a Premarin factory,
a gorgeous Paint girl,
black and white, one of three horses,
along with the mare, Harmony,
and a foster horse that needs training.
The farm is home to any number of rescues:
three sheep, three dogs,
an ebony cat with a litter of gray and striped kittens,
a pony named Elvis, too old to be adopted,
several goats, including one that bleats
like a baby, causing my friend to say,
Oh, Waylon, we hear you.
We could saddle Harmony,
borrow a neighbor's horse and go riding,
but we stand talking until it is too late to ride.
The sun squints through bare alders at the field's margin
where birds begin the evening vespers.
The horses tire of nuzzling our pockets for sugar,
finish the last of the carrots,
and amble away, their swaying, free bodies
unbridled, ungroomed.

Hound

Like a hunter keeps hounds,
I keep a string of angers
chained in a muddy side yard.
They bay righteously,
whine and snuffle, collapse
with clown faces on oversized paws.
Some days a new anger arrives,
a motherless pup
so feckless it would be a mercy
to drown it. I bring it
into the house, nurse it with bottles
of Pablum, put it to bed
swaddled in an old shirt.
Now it adores my scent,
turns on every trail to bound
back to me, grows so huge
it knocks me off my feet.
I want to love it,
but anger is a hound that bays
even when there is no moon.
All it needs is my face
at the window, my nod
of approval, my strangled love.

Hasn't Marriage a Soul?

When they first exchanged vows, it was small.
Marriage was like an aggie, a marble
a boy might carry in his pocket for a charm.

When she took it out again, it had changed,
the same heft, but with a sinister aspect,
bloodless and soft as a rabbit's foot. Later,

it was a pirate's green parrot
kneading her shoulder, nipping at his ear.
When they made love, the marriage shrieked,

flying dizzily about the room. The children
have learned to tease it. They adore
how its hide clatters, its breath of fire.

Her Desk

Rescued from a warehouse
the desk anchors
one corner of my study,

dark altar of books
and framed pictures, candles,
a map. Whose desk

was this before it found me?
Some brittle soul's,
white-haired now, living

in a nursing home—
maybe she, too, was hard to love,
craved quiet more

than husband and children.
Here's the mark where she rested
a cigarette, ash searing

the varnish while she worked
the meter of a villanelle.
Here her thumbnail

teased the grain.
Should I rhyme? She shuffles
the bright corridor,

hums a nocturne.
Under my pen,
the desk, too, hums.

What Clutter Does

Clutter is a metaphor for what it isn't,
for the order you've wanted in your life
all your life. Clutter stands not for things kept,
but for what you couldn't keep, the pickle jars
full of marbles that, for a quarter,
you never could guess the number of,
all the raffles entered and all the marbles lost
through knotholes and behind porch steps,
all the spelling bees you dropped from
in the second round, not because you couldn't spell,
but because you couldn't concentrate
in the clutter of so much noise.
Clutter could stand for Sunday School prizes
for Most Visitors Brought when you
couldn't bring any, your parents' Buick
station wagon with the flip-up jumpseat
in the back already full, as if that was fair,
your messy sisters always scrubbing
down the crayons to dull thumbs.
In your cluttered heart there's a shelf
with nothing on it, a cleared space
where you place your dreams like knick
knacks (that dusty, that quiet),
whenever and wherever the busy world
proves too much for you. When your own
breath is all the clutter you can stand.

Griffin

Living with children, it's in the early hours
that I see Time clearly—
unfriended beast, she sways in a corner,
red eyes oozing. She licks
a sore on one leg, rattles her chains.
If I pause too long
searching the right word, she'll nudge my back,
make her peculiar exhalation of breath,
a snort like a horse's. She can pace here,
though it's awkward, and returning
to her corner requires careful
refolding of tail and wings.

Time's lumpy, furless, an iguana's green today.

She drools and sighs.
I fill my hands with poems,
coax her to eat them.

Unripened

We wade through hip-
       high brambles to find the creek
  running chill and dark
    under vine maple and doug
       fir. Water skippers

crinkle the face of the water.
    Ancient alders nod and grumble
in the breeze. Our feet
  slip on moss-cloaked stones.
      In the widest pool, beavers

have strewn branches—
    torn rags of lichen,
gnawed ends of limbs,
  leaves still green, woven
    through a dam so thin

it is like a sketch of a dam
    and even so already slowing
the slow descent of the creek
  to the river. Our shoes and pantlegs
    dripping, we break a path

around the beavers in hiding.
    We cross through twin-berry
and bear-berry, through cascara
  and sorrel, wild mint
    and goose grass. We wade

nettles and devil's club, thistle
      and tansy. From hip-high
   brambles, we pluck
     fat red berries, so unripe
        they astonish our tongue.

If I'm Not

If I'm not the woman you took me for
then take your pick of women, scoop one

from Earth's bounty, the heart
of a melon, a tomato sweet

off the vine. If irises
in late afternoon recall what you've lost,

if yellow squash sprawls coercive as weeds,
if blue darner dragonflies threaten

to stitch your life back together, then stitch
your life back together. If your eye

falls on me, know that behind me
the women line up, their hair reddish-gold

as if you've stumbled into a Titian portrait.
If your lips must be stung, let them be stung

in the garden, let them be swollen
and honeyed with kisses.

I Could Love You That Way

The way a woman cleans house, tying her hair
in a kerchief, knocking down cobwebs

with a broom. All day gathering clothes
and toys and books from beneath the beds.

Vacuuming under the couch cushions,
scrubbing the drains, polishing

the fixtures. I could love you that way,
methodically, thoroughly, offering my body

at day's end as if it were a house,
as if it were a place for you to lie down.

2. Take Heart

A little bag in my chest held a whirling stone
so hot it was past burning
so radiant it was blinding

—May Swenson

1.

She wakes to find her heart
has sprouted wings, as surprising a thing
as the avocado pit sprouting
in the kitchen window.

How did she come
to this place of fluttering,
the uncertain shimmer
beneath her ribs—a wounded place low
under her left breast—such banging
to get out?

    If she opens the door,
will it rest in her hands, twitching
under her thumbs?

Or will it dart away,
crashing against the light fixture?

She unlatches the door,
extends her hand—

the air is thin, deep in this longing.
If the canary dies, she'll know
to flee,
        carrying her body
            like a birdless cage.

2.

Now that the ladder's gone,
I must lie down where all the ladders start.
—W. B. Yeats

Damp as a bunker, her heart
is a room full of old books.

She loves their deafening quiet.
That ladder, even broken,

will take her to a water view,
to the barred owl's bark and flourish,

to the sun, shaking out the day
like a blanket.

But what good is a ladder,
when the cot has arms, a mouth

to call her name? She lies down,
draws her knees to her chest,

obedient, obeisant
to a fat book's beating heart.

3.

Batter my heart, three-personed God—
that's what Donne begged.
The waitress can't think of battering
without going straight to fish
and chips, chicken-fried steak.

She reads a story about a housewife
serving mouse heart to her husband,
a delicacy the color of a bruise.

But why think of that,
as if her own heart were as small,
wrapped in breadcrumbs?

       An image slipped silent between ribs.

She arranges knife and fork and spoon
beside her face reflected
in a polished plate.

4.

To the extent the heart is iambic,
timed to the body's breath, that's how far
I can dream it. If the world has a dream
it's a dream of the heart, tendrilled, smoke-
charred, walls painted with ideographs
(horses, buffalo, spears).
Each night we lie down with the heart.
We dream a bloody pulse, cave entrance
and long tunnel, symbol of sex,
of sex and birth. It's all desire.
Waking we count to five, open our eyes.
This is the world the heart lends us
as we move through it, chanting.

5.

The marriage over, she still has his name
to contend with—blue ink

entwined with red over her heart.
She could have it removed.

She could put another tattoo over it,
thick braid of snake or smoke.

Her mother suggests dating only
men named David. A new lover jokes

that it spells *damned*.
Each time she crosses her arms

over her blouse and skims it
over her head, she is back there,

swearing before God to be his forever.
His mouth like the artist's needle,

whispering, *I do, I do.*

6.

Heart says, "Stick a fork in me,
I'm done," stomps from the kitchen,
fryer and grill still smoking, tears up
his timecard, curses the boss.
Heart's fed up with being a metaphor,
red rose, target any arrow can find.
He'll no longer be chambered
like a guest house, won't ring like a bell.
Won't stand shyly by like deer in morning mist.
He's finished being lion-hearted,
finished being the *coeur* in courage,
the core of anything.
He won't be deep as the sea,
groaning in chains or out of them,
won't decorate your sleeve,
won't ache, won't break,
won't grow heavy as a stone, won't shatter
like a dropped wine glass.
When you wake in the night
to his terrible knocking, open the door.
Listen.
Let him tell you what he wants.

7.

If my heart skips one beat
it may as well skip two.
Skip three and I'll buy it a jumprope.
If my heart skitters and peeps

it does so for medical reasons—
it's congenital, it's the inconsistency
of age. Does the heart
really say "murmur"

or is that just show for the doctor,
bell of stainless steel pressed
like a lover's ear against one breast?
"Murmur," as if the heart

said "mother" or "sea"
in another language.
What tongue is the heart's tongue?
Not the irrespressible English,

but one clenched before
declensions. I want to press my own ear
to my heart. I want to hear it
murmur, "Love, love."

8.

Her heart
        a running horse
                she sings in a sea

of wither and stifle,
        fetlock and pastern,
                hock and flank,

arching shadows
        trampling the downed
                fences, murmuring

throaty mating
        of horses,
                fields of burdock

and tansy and thistle,
        lip of stars
                in purple crowns,

saved
        until morning—
                salt beyond saying.

9.

Now that I have your heart by heart, I see.
—Louise Bogan

You harrumph and murmur, cup
my chin in your hand like
an egg in a spoon.

Oh, handsome, encumber me
with curt kisses, your abrupt
and cluttered caresses,

petals like chrysanthemums,
sullen anemones, moody
tweeters gleaming

under a dull sea. Flabbergast me
with lollipops. Give an oily
shudder. So humanly

human, slumping
against my shoulder, chuckling
like a loon.

10.

Not the heart, but maybe
the liver. Why not love you

with my whole pancreas?
My thalamus adores you. My cochlea

lies awake all night, filled with you
as if with an inner sea.

My knees ache, pursuing you
with the runner's pure desire.

My heart withdraws, abbess
dedicated to her four chambers,

praying for purer thoughts.
loving only a huge and bodiless God.

11.

A yellowing archetype, pale against a row
of hot pink symbols. Silver leaves of a metaphor

translucent in noon sun—simile and simulacrum,
hyperbole, laced ironies, a blasted paradox.

Late-bloomed beneath the crabapple,
a quartet of metaphysical conceits. Bees bumble

among tall metonymies. Striped allusions
climb a synesthetic rose. Blue rhymes.

12.

February, early morning, three red-winged blackbirds
perched on cattails in the marsh.

Three red-winged blackbirds like three black notes
arranged on a measure of music.

A love poem of only three words.
Three red-winged blackbirds. February morning.

13.

Her heart unfolds, a blue heron
        standing one-legged in a roadside ditch.
                Opening like a jackknife
        it flies straight into the horizon,

huge wings hinged, legs trailing,
        until it's no more than a dot
                at the end of a sentence.
        No words occur to call it back.

Can she jiggle her liver
        like a herring, or croak like a frog?
                She crouches amid crumpled
        coffee cups, cellophane wrappers,

spent cigarettes. *Take wing,*
        she whispers, a peculiar
                incantation of the verb—

        as if she had said, *Take heart.*

3. Living in Books

The page my acre

—May Swenson

To Begin

Somewhere someone has to make a beginning.
It has to be made out of nothing
or out of a landscape utterly other,
of trees bent in the wind as if with the want
of what begins.

So a pumpkin seed is planted, or the door
on a birdcage closed, or all the birds let go.
Thoreau plants his nine bean rows.
Anna Karenina slips into a party dress.
Gulliver wakes to find himself bound
by a thousand threads,
though by the time he sits up, breaking them,
it has already begun.

In the beginning, nothing so very large.
A raindrop streaks a window pane. A leaf falls.
A horse is saddled. An alarm clock ticks toward five a.m.

Here is our beginning,
back in the dark, back at the quiet gesture—
a hand cupping a breast, a baby's cry.
A boy stoops to pick up a feather,
a girl swings her leg over the horse's back,
the alarm sings.

Like a bride, you wake to find yourself bound,
your white dress woven of so many threads
you can't tear them away.

Don't cry. It's your story.
Take it in your hands. Begin.

Into the Ice

for Bruce

You are reading a book about explorers in Greenland,
a plane crash, a glacier, crevasses. It's a long book,

and night after night, when I would so much rather read
to myself, my very sweet novel about love

and marriage, you lean on one elbow and say,
Listen to this. A drop off, a misstep,

a psychotic episode brought on by starvation,
limbs eaten away with frostbite. After a time, your explorers

are found, but the book doesn't end—
bad weather makes rescue impossible, food

has to be parachuted in, warm boots and parkas.
More food. Over the long winter one survivor puts on

so much weight he can no longer crawl from the shelter.
I listen to you read (my book, still open on my lap)

and I see how it's all about love and marriage,
how our daughters, growing up,

have marooned us here together, thrown us back
on our own meager resources. I knew you

once, decades ago, before Greenland, before the airplane,
before the glacier. The bed is a vast ice field.

I pull on my boots and begin the long trek back to you.
Your sonorous voice, my only guide.

Like Protecting Wings

Daughters shout, slam doors, dance through glittering rain,
hot sparks on pink tongues. In our Mother Goose no Humpty
Dumpty lolls, golden yolk up. No tin soldiers clatter
bayonets. No horses champ or chomp on no white
hills. There is nothing we can't put right—
broken plates, dowsed candles, spilled
milk, mateless socks. Cut fingers bleed
spangled hearts. We keep a hen not
for omelets but for her cerise
feathers, her comic wattle
and waddle. Peas in a pod,
we wash our feet in gin,
adore midnights quickened
with ravens, fix constellations
in our hair, wear gloves
of feathers, sport
epaulets like
protecting
wings.

Fabled

After the mouse took the thorn
from his paw, the lion was grateful,
though not so much that he swore off mice
forever. So it is when love begins.
He says he'd never harm her.
She says she'll never love another.
It's too good to be true.
Human nature turns out to be bigger
than happily-ever-afters.
God knows, it lasts longer.
He yells. She loves the baby more.
He's a brute. She's a shrew.
If you loved me, she says.
Fortunately, I don't, he answers,
and in the shocked
or hurt or smug silence after
you can hear the mouse in the lion's teeth,
bones crunching delicately
as thin crusts on a favorite dessert.

Insomnia

That summer a long friendship ended
and I couldn't sleep. I was reading
a biography of Virginia Woolf
and I had a sense of myself as no longer
inside my own life. My husband must have
felt it, too, both of us drawing back like horses
from an unfamiliar stir in the grass.
In the last hours of night I would rise,
and though it was early, I'd make a cup
of coffee and sit outside under the stars,
whose light reached me as a kind of afterthought.
Virginia had insomnia, too.
When I did sleep, I dreamed I was young again,
and just conflicts setting out on my tangled path.

English Café

for Ann Harrington

She greets us with a simile,
the daily specials listed on her oversized thesis.
Will you have regular or irregular verbs?

My friend orders braised clause
with a side of apostrophes. I choose
small plates of articles and prepositions.

But no dative? the waitress asks,
No genitive? She offers Shakespeare
or D. H. Lawrence for dessert.

We sip from snifters of Strunk & White,
share adverbs while coordinating
conjunctions rise languidly

to dance. Between parentheses,
a gerund cracks jokes. We pay
in participles, tip a metaphor.

You've forgotten your predicate,
the waitress calls after us, dangling
a modifier on a ring of rhymed nouns.

If Plot Is What Happens

then what about those long, still moments
when nothing happens? When you

don't leave the room, don't slam
the door, don't raise your voice,

not even your hand? When you sit,
quiet, unmoving, almost unthinking?

Maybe you're reading. Maybe you've come
to the end of the page and instead of turning

the page, you don't turn it, letting the plot
tick to a halt like a clock winding down.

The stray seconds sweep over you,
nearly invisible, lake water you swam in

as a child, where, looking up to see the sun
press its hands to the lake's surface,

you knew, *This is the part where nothing happens.*
Except you pushed upward, breaking through—

and the world swung into motion,
its plot dizzy and dazzling around you.

Invitation

You see it late at night on television
       all the time. Perhaps someone's wife
            comes back as a dog—
      of course there's no sex,

just some very sweet dancing
       toward the movie's end when the crotchety
            old survivor is worn down.
      Or maybe the departed loved one's a ghost,

maybe he inhabits some other person's body,
       (the more absurd the better—
            Whoopi Goldberg French-kissing
      some white chick, but really

Whoopi is that dead guy
       so it's all *hetero* and nothing to upset
            the big C conservatives).
      Grandfathers come back, grumbling

at the interruption, and sisters, too,
       giving parenting advice (it's always
            the better mom who dies, TV requires it).
      But no matter how wise they've grown,

grappling with death, the dead
       have conflicts left over.
            So whichever way it goes,
      art imitating life, or life, art—

why shouldn't you come?
       It is almost the anniversary of your death.
            I've set a place at the table.
      You've got some explaining to do.

When Poems Sit Vacant

When poems sit vacant for a long time,
they can attract squatters.
> —real-estate story misheard on KUOW

An old poem will suit best, maybe Aphra Beyn
or a lyric by Sappho, something with the doors
falling askew from their hinges. A poem only a few
decades forgotten will do. Avoid the ones

too often anthologized, and the herds
of college freshmen tramping through.
Find a capacious poem, if not in lines then in depth,
a poem with secret crannies. Windows,

even broken, will let in the light. I can recommend
an obscure sonnet by Gerard Manley Hopkins,
quiet as a monastery, or a verse by Edna
St. Vincent Millay with long porches and shade.

Pull a rocking chair out to that porch.
If the sun isn't shining, no matter. Being alone
in the lines will be enough. Smell the rain.
Listen to the thunder of the sweet old rhymes.

What She Wanted to Put in Her Poem

When he decided to end it all, he took his pistol
to the garden and held the muzzle to his ear.

His brains would fertilize the cucumbers,
the heirloom tomatoes, the white flesh

of the onions. His blood would seep from him
into the soil where the beans drifted over their stakes.

He would waste nothing.
Through the kitchen window, his wife

and step-daughters watched. *The son of a bitch
is nothing but a coward,* his wife said.

He couldn't hear what they said.
But he lowered the pistol. He sank to his knees.

Divorce followed. Years of apartments. Jobs
not worthy of his genius. His younger stepdaughter

still remembers him standing in the garden.
She remembers how dark the soil, how green

the plants. A mist of rain, so light, adorning
his head like a halo. How brave he was, is what

she thinks (holding a pen, staring at the white page),
to have stood from there and walked

back into his life, not knowing what it would hold,
whether bounty or lack.

Marrying the Villain

Even in my dreams we marry in a garden,
pond full of rushes and swans,
the call of blackbirds.
Dressed in rose petals, the bridesmaids
are my sisters and not my sisters.
Your groomsmen and the minister stand waiting
beneath the arbor with such an air
of expectation that I don't know
which I should marry.
In life, the wedding music
was voices and a guitar.
The dream drags out a baby grand,
puddle of reflecting light,
notes dripping a brooding, lavender Bach.
At our wedding, you refused to dance,
and I cheerfully did without, but if
our marriage were a novel, that would be
the moment when the heroine's heart
chips open, a crack like a door ajar.
The dream insists on dancing—
pushes me into the arms of a masked bandit
who waltzes me down a hillside
slick with goose droppings and buttercups.
My white dress lifts around us,
a flock of whistling swans.

Living in Books

Too much conformity turns you into a giant bug.
Your mother wears a scarlet letter.
If she abandons you, it's to become a notorious Madame,
a morphine addict who dies in the snow,
a naïve swimmer crossing the gulf of Mexico.

In literature, perdition is absolute.

Your boss goes hunting a white whale
and you have to go with him.
Your husband sets his mind for California
and you're up all night, burning
your mother's letters in the woodstove.

After a storm, angels litter the backyard.
You might be an angel,
you might be a demon vampire,
your life borrowed, allusory,
posed in period costume like a doll.
Bullets stop where the white space begins,
life and death frozen at your leaden feet.
Your mysterious neighbor's a bootlegger,
a war hero in love with your cousin, a gorilla.

To be safe, check "all of the above."

You thought it an accident that you moved here
to this house, to this town, at this time?
Nothing, dear reader, is accidental.
A new point of view, another chapter, a whole new life
lies waiting with every turned page—

after your death, your author will still prod you
like a macabre puppet out of your grave.
"When I died," you'll whisper,
the window sill buzzing with trapped flies.

Why We Write

Before he died, your brother wrote down a story
about a boy who plucked a lime from a tree outside a cave

and went into the cave holding the lime
like a torch. In his faith, the lime became a torch

and by its light he made his way deeply
into the earth. That was his story, just that,

he was no Orpheus, though his wife had left him
and he did want her back. He didn't have the children

with him, of course, though he wasn't drugging
anymore, not even drinking. This was, you remember,

a long time ago, before we had computers
in every house, before cable TV. Before cell phones.

Though maybe he listened to music, listened
and wrote his stories down. So, a type of Orpheus.

Your brother couldn't spell worth a damn.
He wasn't a great storyteller. But he wrote down

a few stories. When his wife left him,
she took even the light fixtures. And though his death

was an accident, and he couldn't have seen it coming,
 he must have plucked that lime

in a flood of consciousness. He must have known
that he would need a bitter light to guide him.

4. What World, in Our Becoming

How will it be
to lie in the sky
without roof or door
and wind for an eye

—May Swenson

Sleep

Like sleep, death   demands unhooking,
unsnapping, unzipping,   pulling off our clothes
like tack from horses   after long roads and dusty fields.
We lie down unbridled   unsaddled, unharnessed,
unyoked. Fed and curried,   bedding turned back,
the mystery left facedown   on the nightstand.
So we ready the body   for dreams that will ride us
bareback, nothing but   wind in our teeth.

What World, in Our Becoming

for Glenda Lewis

What if everything Isaiah and Jesus
and St. John and my mother
said about heaven were only metaphor?
What if the redeemed won't be alone there
or the lion lose its taste for the lamb—
but it was only a way of saying
that heaven is a place of safety?
Not always day and "no more night,"
but only so stunningly different
from what we know that a figure of speech
for "indescribable" is the only way to describe it?
In the womb the infant becomes itself,
forming nose and eye, tongue and ear,
all estranged from need
in its cramped world of salt water,
products of the body's longing for air and light.
How cramped is this world
compared to the next?
When the Apostle Paul said,
"Now I see as through a glass darkly,"
wasn't he making a promise of clarity to come?
What do we long for, not only great shampoo
and excellent deodorant, the perfect beer,
but maybe compassion, maybe peace and plenty.
What would these look like—
one hand in another? Jars of tomatoes
arranged on a shelf? A sword
beaten into a plowshare? What world,
in our becoming, do we now create?

How Stories Go

The town had a legend about that couple,
how during her first marriage she lay nights
in her bed, holding her hand
through the open window sash
where he knelt among peonies
and the Martha Washington roses.
Circumstances changed
(though how, you never knew),
they married, grew old together,
became your friend's grandmother
and step-grandfather. She had the white
almost blue hair of certain elegant
old ladies. He sported a rogue's reputation,
despite dentures, despite the comb-over.
They kept elaborate flowerbeds
and even at the end of October when you stood
at their front door in the dark,
late asters nodded like romantic ghosts.
You said, "Trick or Treat"
and she smiled, dropped a store-bought candy
into your bag (as he loomed
like Dracula over her shoulder).
So you stop your car today and say to your children,
"The couple who lived in that house
had the most beautiful flowers."
The house is abandoned.
Through one smashed window a bramble
stretches its hopeful hand.

The Soul, Lifting

His neck slashed, the murdered man
staggered from the bed
to the dresser and stood, astonished,
where each night for thirty years
he had emptied his pockets of coins and keys—
staring into the mirror
as his life drained from him,
his soul draped like a pair of silk stockings
over his wife's vanity table,
after a while lifting and drifting
into the afterlife without him.

Her Dream of Winter

In her dream of winter
she unravels a yellow sun
heavy as damask, books passage
as if wind were a sleigh,
loneliness a bearskin
to wrap over her knees.
She takes winter by the throat,
shakes loose hail like white teeth,
unfurls a carpet of snow.
She dreams white mountains
where trees crook like candy canes
under a burden of ice,
dreams wool skirts,
thick stockings, long walks
under frozen skies.
In her dream she comes home
to a simmering stew,
to dark bread fresh from the oven,
so hot it melts the snow
from the windowsills.
Hers is a dream without frozen armies,
without children shivering
under thin blankets.
In her dream of winter
even the howling of wolves
rises tender as blue notes
into a sky strung with stars.
If the stars are hard,
they are hard like gems.
She unbraids her hair,
lifts up on her toes
like a jewelry box dancer,
skates across ice
unruffled as a mirror.

When He Thought of Peace

Not the opposite of war
but like the letter
he carried in his pocket.
The rustle of it
over his heart, even when
bullets flew and mud
of the trench crept
over his boots, a letter
he might open wide enough
to let himself inside.
Just holding it, unopened,
just imagining the words
scrawled across the white page,
he could hear birds singing
in the branches of trees,
he could smell spring and blossoms,
see the eagle lift from the tallest fir
on the hill above his father's farm.
That was peace,
to be that boy again,
the eagle bearing what it held
in its talons not like prey,
but as if to a place of safety.

Legs Thin as Branches

The muse when it is new
wobbles on legs thin as branches.
It bleats and mewls,

not a horse to be ridden,
only another baby
needing milk and love.

You have to believe in what isn't there
a long time before it begins
to be there. Years pass

before you dare put a saddle
on its back, before you dare
climb up and weigh the reins

in your hands. When it is new,
the muse teaches you
to practice faith in the music

of what you cannot hear,
to make art of what you cannot see.
When the day dawns

for you to trust your weight
to it, sit up straight. Gather all
that its long becoming

has brought forth in you.
Look steadily in the direction
you must go.

What Didn't Happen

after Wislawa Szymborska's "Could Have"

This is the horse you couldn't catch.
He was a sorrel, a buckskin, a bay,
a paint, a dappled gray.

You should have caught him.
You could never have caught him.

He was yours. He wasn't yours.

He was in the wrong barn. He was in the far field.
You lost him because you hurried.
You lost him because you were slow.

Because unlucky. Because lucky.
Because you hadn't an apple.
Because it was apple time and he was glutted with apples.
Because sunshine spooked him.
Because it rained buckets.

That you carried a bridle, a saddle, a handful of oats—
none of that mattered.
Not boots or hat, not prayers, songs, tears.
The purity of your love didn't matter.
Your virgin heart. Your heart a whore.

And what if you had caught him—
by the mane, by the forelock, by one black hoof,
one white star?

The bridle was beautiful, inlaid with silver.
I'm amazed, too, that he wasn't yours.
But imagine, how far behind, riding,
      you would have left me.

In your ears, a thunder of hooves.

What I Need Now

I need a version of creation
        to account for the cat's curiosity,
                the dog's fidelity, the beauty
      of two white birds flying

over the bare oaks in a field,
        the goat's lust. Humans, it's said,
                are created with a soul,
      on a higher plane than animals,

but where is the soul of the human
        emptying an ashtray on the grass,
                or the soul of the corporation
      building a parking lot on a wetland?

If life is a spiritual quest,
        why do I keep searching
                for the perfect haircut, a sweater
      that will match my eyes?

In the cosmic, Zen sense
        of what use is television?
                Of what use is war? I know
      that I should have asked these questions

eons back, and by now made some
        progress toward answers. Instead it is
                the burro pastured by the trailer park
      who teaches me to mingle my breath

with the morning mist, to love
        the grass because it is,
      as much as because it is a gift
        from any god.

Her Heart, Her Soul

Gray whale. Gray
cat asleep under the bed.
Violet-green swallow

darting into its nest
beneath the eaves
of the house. One bright

feather. What if the soul
is no more than these? Less—
the colors of sunset

reflected in water, foam
on a horse's lip after a gallop.
Vestigial, intransigent.

Or like a verb, not to lie down,
but to lay one's burden down.
The soul always transitive,

possessing, possessed by.
The sea a frayed blanket.
The birdhouse not caring

whether the wren
returns or a squirrel.
The apple tree sheltering

its crop of vipers.

Acknowledgments

Grateful acknowledgments to the editors, staff, and readers of the following print and on-line journals and anthologies where many of these poems first appeared: *Bellingham Review; Bird's Thumb; A Cadence of Hooves: A Celebration of Horses; Calyx, a Journal of Art and Literature for Women; Cairn; Cheat River Review; Cider Press Review; Crosscurrents; Cumberland River Review; Del Sol; Escape into Life (EIL); Five Willows; Floating Bridge Review; Footbridge above the Waterfall* (forthcoming from Rose Alley Press); *Gravel; Message in a Bottle; New Media; Permafrost; One Sentence Poems; Poetry Northwest; Pontoon; Right Hand Pointing; Santa Clara Review; Silver Birches; Stringtown; Superstition Review; Timber Creek Review; Twisted Vine; World Peace Poets*, vols. 1 and 2.

The epigraphs from May Swenson are from *Nature: Poems Old and New* (Houghton Mifflin, 1994).

A portion of the profits from sales of this book will be donated to Ellen Felsenthal's New Moon Farm Goat Rescue & Sanctuary (www.newmoonfarm.org).

Many many thanks to Koon Woon and Goldfish Press, without whose encouragement and attention this book would not exist.

CPSIA information can be obtained
at www.ICGtesting.com
Printed in the USA
FSHW02n0808020918
51972FS